4 FOUR FOUNDATIONAL HABITS OF A DREAM BUILDER

CHRISTINE GIBSON, PH.D.

DREAM BUILDERS UNIVERSITY

Four Foundational Habits of a Dream Builder
By Christine Gibson, Ph.D.
Copyright © 2024 by LaMarqué D. Ward Sr., M.Ed.
Published by Dream Builders University Press
ISBN 978-1-947490-21-5
Graphic Design: Aaron J. Ratzlaff

TABLE OF CONTENTS

Standards 4

Welcome 5

Objectives 5

Be Present 6
    Time To Dream 8
    Vocabulary 10
    Case Study 11
    Activity 12

Be Engaged & Have Fun 13
    Time To Dream 14
    Vocabulary 16
    Case Study 17
    Activity 18

Be A Bucket Filler 19
    Time To Dream 20
    Vocabulary 22
    Case Study 23
    Activity 24

Personal Accountability 25
    Time To Dream 26
    Vocabulary 28
    Case Study 29
    Activity 30

Glossary 31

References 32

Standards for Dream Builders University Four Foundational Habits of a Dream Builder

Ohio Learning Standards

GRADES 4-5

RI.4.1 Refer to details and examples in a text when explaining what the text says explicitly and when drawing inferences from the text.

RI.5.1 Quote accurately from a text when explaining what the text says explicitly and when drawing inferences from the text.

GRADES 6-8

RI.6.1 Cite textual evidence to support analysis of what the text says explicitly as well as inferences drawn from the text.

RI.7.1 Cite several pieces of textual evidence to support analysis of what the text says explicitly as well as inferences drawn from the text.

RI.8.1 Cite the textual evidence that most strongly supports an analysis of what the text says explicitly as well as inferences drawn from the text.

GRADES 9-12

RI.9-10.1 Cite strong and thorough textual evidence to support analysis of what the text says explicitly as well as inferences drawn from the text.

RI.11-12.1 Cite strong and thorough textual evidence to support analysis of what the text says explicitly as well as inferences drawn from the text, including determining where the text leaves matters uncertain.

SEL Standards

SELF-AWARENESS

Grade 3-5- A4. 1.b Identify and describe how personal choices and behavior impacts self and others

Middle Grades- A4. 1.c Describe how personal responsibility is linked to being accountable for one's choices and behavior

High School- A4. 1.d Demonstrate internalization of personal responsibility and being accountable as one prepares for postsecondary life

SELF-MANAGEMENT

Grade 3-5- B2. 4.b Identify alternative strategies with guidance toward a specified goal

Middle Grades- B2. 4.c Monitor progress toward a specified goal by developing checkpoints and adjusting the plan or action steps as needed

High School- B2. 4.d Evaluate progress toward achieving a specified goal and re-evaluate or adapt the plan or action steps as needed

SOCIAL AWARENESS

Grades 3-5- C1. 3.b Demonstrate empathetic reactions in response to others' feelings and emotions

Middle Grades- C1. 3.c Demonstrate empathy through understanding of others' feelings and acknowledgement of their perspective

High School- C1. 3.d Demonstrate empathy through compassion in self and encourage in others

RELATIONSHIP SKILLS

Grades 3-5- D3. 3.b Generate ideas to reach a compromise and find resolution during conflict

Middle Grades- D3. 3.c Exchange ideas and negotiate solutions to resolve conflicts, seeking support when needed

High School- D3. 3.d Utilize problem-solving resources and supports to facilitate conflict resolution, recognizing that seeking help is a strength

RESPONSIBLE DECISION-MAKING

Grades 3-5- E2. 3.b Predict possible future outcomes of personal actions in various settings

Middle Grades- E2. 3.c Utilize knowledge of outcomes to inform future decisions

High School- E2. 3.d Integrate prior experience and knowledge of outcomes to inform future decisions

WELCOME!

Welcome to **The Four Foundational Habits of a Dream Builder**. This curriculum introduces a balanced approach to developing the capacity to build a better you while creating positive relationships and breaking barriers.

This Interactive Guide to the The Four Foundational Habits is a great instrument that supports a balanced approach to building relationships cross-culturally and across socioeconomic boundaries. The Four Habits and the 5 Social and Emotional Learning skills that are outlined in this tool are designed to deliver the best results when used in a setting where dialogue is welcomed, and collaboration is encouraged.

OBJECTIVES

- The student will identify the Four Foundational Habits.

- The student will recognize how the Four Foundational Habits support Social and Emotional development.

- The student will recognize the importance of their identities.

- The student will understand the value of having a balanced perspective.

- The student will create ways to make a positive impact in their homes, schools, and communities.

- The student will demonstrate ways to overcome obstacles and challenges and keep a positive mindset.

Be Present

What does it mean to be present? How do you show up in spaces and be there for others? What does it take to be there, show up and be present in that moment? Why is it important to be present?

You must consider these questions to show up in order to be fully present. As a part of your development, a person must be nurtured. A portion of being nurtured is having someone being there for you and showing up for you. Now, this can happen in different ways; this can be both physical, mental, and spiritual. Being present and exercising your ability to be mindful makes you happier. It may also help you deal with pain more effectively, decrease your stress, reduce its impact on your health, and increase your ability to cope with negative emotions like fear and anger.

To Be Present is the glue that brings people together.

However, let's not forget how your identity, thoughts, and actions are a huge part of how you are able to be there for yourself and others. Understanding who you are and the power you possess is essential. Social and Emotional Wellness supports how we, as humans understand:

1. Who we are

2. Our ability to be present

3. Why we make individual choices

4. Our connection with others

5. How we self-discipline

6. And how we thrive in different social environments

Understanding the importance of yourself helps you to be there for others. The power of showing up and being there for yourself can help balance how you show up for others. Applying a balanced approach to building relationships supports all involved. This is why You matter so much in the process of being there, and being present.

Idioms by **The Free Dictionary** defines **Be There** - To provide or be available to provide support to one.

Positive Psychology defines **Self-Awareness** as the ability to see yourself clearly and objectively through reflection and introspection.

CASEL defines **Self-Awareness** as the ability to understand one's own emotions, thoughts, and values and how they influence behaviors across contexts.

CASEL defines **Relationship Skills** as the abilities to establish and maintain healthy relationships and to effectively navigate settings with diverse individuals and groups.

In other words, **Relationship Skills** are the ability, skills, trust, tools, knowledge, knowing, and understanding to create, communicate, evolve, grow, and maintain a relationship.

Here are some ways to

Be Present

for others:

- Listen attentively
- Have empathy
- Don't just listen to respond, but understand
- Validate others' feelings
- Expand your perspective
- You don't have a solution or an opinion
- Offer support if you can

As individuals, we embark on a journey to understand ourselves while considering our environment. Who are your influencers? To what extent do these individuals and groups play a role in defining one's self and the perceptions of others? Your perception and ideas of self may determine how you weigh in on so many vital issues. And how you view yourself also influences how you view others. This may limit or advance your ability to be fully present.

The culture in which you emerged or grew up, your experiences, and your lack of experiences mold you into the individuals you are. These are all factors you need to consider when defining yourself. Again, how you view yourselves plays a significant part in how you view others. Your lived experiences and the experiences of individuals close to us play a huge factor in how you perceive yourself, your political views, how you see individuals in differing social and economic classes, and the degree to which you accept others of diverse backgrounds. Again, all these factors must be considered as you begin your journey to **Be There**!

Be Present

Understanding the value of you and your own identity supports understanding the importance of the identities of others. This value system creates a ripple effect. In order to be fully present, you must recognize and appreciate the significance of mattering. Knowing you matter helps you to be there for yourself and be there for others. Drawing from Dr. Bettina L. Love's brilliantly written work titled, We Want To Do More Than Survive gives a deeper meaning to why we as individuals must matter.

TIME TO DREAM

- What is something you are good at?

- How can being open-minded help you to be present?

- Are you there for yourself? If so, in what ways?

- Is it possible to not be there for yourself, but for others? What are some possible effects of this?

- Are you defining others' expectations based on your own experiences?

"I learned above all else to protect my dignity. My dignity was never to be compromised, which meant never compromising my voice and my connection to how I mattered in this world. When you compromise your voice, you compromise your dignity. No dignity, no power. Knowing I had a voice backed by common sense, which I understood was supposed to be used to protect myself, was one of the most powerful things I have ever been taught."

Dr. Bettina L. Love

Being fully present for others builds and strengthens relationships. It also supports you as an individual by knowing that you can support and nurture others in ways that are also important to you.

Why is being there for yourself important?

_____

_____

_____

_____

How can being Self-Aware help you to Be Present for others?

_____
_____
_____
_____

Think of a situation when someone was confiding in you but you were not fully present. What are some reasons this may happen?

_____
_____
_____
_____

List some ways you have been there for others?

_____
_____
_____
_____

In what ways can a person's childhood affect their ability to Be Present for others?

_____
_____
_____
_____

Be Present

VOCABULARY

Review the vocabulary and definitions and create your own sentence to help you better understand the terms.

word	sentence

The Four Foundational Habits of a Dream Builder

CASE STUDY

Christine was not having such a great day. Christine is a junior at Dream Builders High School. She didn't complete her homework, which was extremely important for her to get a passing grade in her History class. She was up all night trying to figure out how she could come up with the money to pay for her "perfect outfit" for the dance that was coming up in four days. Although she knew how important this homework was, she was not focused enough to get it all done. When she got to school the next day, her best friend Blake told Christine that he really needed to talk to her because he was having some issues with his parents. Blake and his parents had been arguing for weeks and "something very bad happened" according to Blake. Christine was really not in the mood and did not want to listen to Blake complain about his parents again, but she stood there and listened.

Get in a group or with a partner and unpack this case study.

What should Christine do? Is it okay for Christine not to listen to Blake? How can Christine be there for Blake? Is it possible for Christine to be there for herself and Blake? What are some healthy steps Christine can take that would be best in this situation and would help Christine's relationship with Blake?

_____

_____

_____

_____

_____

_____

_____

_____

_____

_____

_____

_____

Be Present

ACTIVITY ✎

Design a flier that will spark conversations and support how to Be Present for yourself and others.

Be Engaged & Have Fun

A considerable part of growing and learning is developed through play.

Being Engaged & Having Fun can help you tap into your natural way to be creative, enthusiastic, and having fun. This is the spirit that drives the curious mind.

The goal is to bring this mindset to everything you do.

When you have a mindset to be engaged and have fun, it's easier to achieve serious goals if you have fun doing them. Sharing moments of enjoyment with peers builds camaraderie and trust. A fun approach encourages yourself and your peers to be genuine and friendly.

While having fun is an essential part of being creative, it is just as necessary to manage oneself for this to be effective. Self-Management can help you know when the situation may need creativity or a more serious tone. Being able to discipline yourself and manage your thoughts and behaviors may help keep your environment healthy and upbeat. Knowing your personal boundaries and the boundaries of others can support respecting one another through play and work.

Being mindful and socially aware of your environments and various settings you are in may also aid in respecting boundaries and understanding a respectful way to be creative and incorporate healthy play. Being Engaged & Having Fun is more meaningful when you value others' perspectives and understand that what may be fun, playful, and creative to some may devalue others.

Fun is defined as Engaging in activities for enjoyment and recreation rather than a serious or practical purpose.

CASEL defines **Self-Management** as the abilities to manage one's emotions, thoughts, and behaviors effectively and to achieve goals and aspirations.

Being Engaged & Having Fun

can be helpful to:

- Use humor to make people feel included.

- Invite (not demand) peers to join in fun activities.

- Know your team's boundaries.

- Experiment with new ideas to improve results.

- See mistakes as an opportunity to learn.

Be Engaged & Have Fun

TIME TO DREAM

- How can having fun be helpful at school?

- Why is it important to incorporate into challenging situations?

- Why are setting boundaries important?

- Discuss a time when having fun went wrong and others were not considered.

CASEL defines **Social Awareness** as the ability to understand the perspective and socialize with others, including those from diverse backgrounds, cultures, and contexts.

Dictionary Oxford Languages defines **Self-Discipline** as the ability to control one's feelings and overcome one's weaknesses; the ability to pursue what one thinks is right despite temptations to abandon it.

Play can bring joy to a difficult situation. Play may also allow a much-needed break from the seriousness of daily tasks. However, it is extremely important to know when the situation calls for less playfulness when boundaries are set.

Being Socially Aware may support:

▶ Understanding others' perspectives.

▶ Demonstrating empathy and compassion.

▶ Understanding the influences of organizations and systems on behavior.

▶ Recognizing the importance of expressing gratitude.

▶ Showing compassion and concern for others' feelings.

Now that you have a broader understanding of **Being Engaged & Having Fun**, let's answer a few questions.

How does knowing your environment support healthy fun/play?

_____
_____
_____
_____

What are some things you need to consider when incorporating fun activities?

_____
_____
_____

Name some ways being engaged & having fun can support you? Explain your answer.

_____
_____
_____

How can mistakes be used as an opportunity for growth?

_____
_____
_____

Describe a way you can use fun/play to have a positive impact at school and at home.

_____
_____
_____

Why is it important to use self-management skills when incorporating fun activities?

_____
_____
_____

Be Engaged & Have Fun

VOCABULARY

Review the vocabulary and definitions and create your own sentence to help you better understand the terms.

word	sentence

CASE STUDY

Gina and three of her classmates worked on a group project in science class. Gina's partners were Kajai, Terri, and Juan. They were all tenth-grade students and attended Ward STEM High School. They were working on creating a sustainable community garden. As they brainstormed ideas, Terri thought of a way to make a market stand in front of a local supermarket in a neighborhood whose residents struggled to find fresh produce. This neighborhood had been known for having older, run-down homes and was just not the prettiest sight. However, it was also known for having incredible people. As Terri explained his ideas, Gina interrupted and said, "We should have a dodgeball game with the vegetables we grow. If they get hit in the head with lettuce, they can take it home and eat it. They are used to eating off the ground anyways."

Gina began to laugh when she noticed Kajai with her head down. Kajai and her family lived in the neighborhood Gina was joking about. This joke made Kajai feel less than the others in the group. Juan looked at Gina and said, "That joke was not funny but offensive." Gina shrugged her shoulders and said, "Well, it was funny to me."

Get in a group or with a partner and unpack this case study.

What could Gina have done differently? What assumptions were made in this scenario? How can the group support Kajai? How can the group support Gina in being more mindful?

_____
_____
_____
_____
_____
_____
_____
_____
_____
_____
_____

Be Engaged & Have Fun

ACTIVITY ✎

Create a campaign that supports building a sustainable community space for your classroom or school building that calls for Equity. Make sure it is inclusive of individuals and groups that are not similar to yours. Add healthy **Fun** into this activity while working. Include persons and groups that may support your campaign. You may also create a vision board that showcases your goal(s) for building sustainable communities. Be sure to include your goal on your vision board with visuals and words representing your purpose. HAVE FUN!

Be a Bucket Filler

What does it mean to make someone's day? What does it take to make someone's day?

Being a Bucket Filler means finding simple ways to serve or delight people in a meaningful, memorable way. It's about contributing to someone else's life—not because you want something, but because that's the person you want to be.

Every interaction is a chance to make a positive impact. Everyone wants to be appreciated and acknowledged. Simple gestures make a more significant impact when they come from your heart. When you brighten someone's day, you receive a gift that gives meaning and purpose to your life.

These moments should be thoughtful when you choose to make someone's day.

Making a responsible decision by being mindful and anticipating the reaction of others are respectful ways to Make Their Day.

Here are some ways to
Be a Bucket Filler

- Write a thank you note.
- "Catch" peers doing good things.
- Encourage a peer or family member.
- Take that extra step someone doesn't expect.
- Celebrate successes.

CASEL defines **Responsible Decision-Making** as the abilities to make caring and constructive choices about personal behavior and social interaction across diverse situations.

Responsible Decision-Making supports Make Their Day by:

- Making responsible decisions after considering the facts or evidence.
- Identifying solutions for both personal and social challenges.
- Evaluate the consequences of your choices.
- Understanding the importance of critical thinking skills.

Be a Bucket Filler

TIME TO DREAM

- Describe a time when you made someone's day.

- Has someone ever made your day? Explain.

- Discuss a time when an attempt to make someone's day backfired.

- Why are friendly, small gestures so important?

Being a Bucket Filler is being aware of your choices as an individual and their impact on others. Responsible Decision-Making also supports the consideration of others when making these decisions. A part of making someone's day is being able to self-evaluate when making choices. You may have to consider others before making your choices. Your choice to make someone's day may take you out of your comfort zone if this is something that is not familiar to you. These are things to consider when deciding how or what you will do to make someone's day. Sometimes decisions are made because individuals feel a sense of safety within their choices (physically safe and psychologically safe). However, what is considered safe for one person may not be safe for others.

Self-evaluation and self-reflection are critical as you examine the importance of making accountable choices. You must also consider ethical responsibility when making decisions and identify possible challenges within your choices.

Nonetheless, a simple smile, a head nod, a thumbs up, or an affirming note are all grand gestures when your goal is to Make Their Day.

Name three possible positive outcomes from Being a Bucket Filler.

1. _____
   _____

2. _____
   _____

3. _____
   _____

The Four Foundational Habits of a Dream Builder

Explain why it is important to take into consideration others' feelings and values before making a choice to do something nice.

_____
_____
_____
_____
_____
_____

How can making someone's day, make your day?

_____
_____
_____
_____
_____
_____

What are some benefits to self-reflecting and considering others? Explain.

_____
_____
_____
_____
_____
_____
_____

Be a Bucket Filler

VOCABULARY

Review the vocabulary and definitions and create your own sentence to help you better understand the terms.

word	sentence

CASE STUDY

Kameron, a seventeen-year-old and a senior at Carter High School, decided to do something nice for the entire senior class. He had a part-time job working at a bakery in his neighborhood so he did not have a lot of money to spend. He decided to write a note to everyone in his senior class. After school, Kameron went to the store, bought a double pack of sticky notes, and wrote a note to all seniors. He really wanted to personalize each note, but he didn't know everyone personally. So he decided to write, "I love you, and I wish you the best of luck" on all the notes.

The next day, Kameron woke up early and was one of the first students in the school. He began putting the notes on the lockers of all the seniors. He felt good about what he had done.

As the students entered the building, he heard some seniors saying, "who wrote me this stupid love note." Some of the seniors balled theirs up and threw them at each other. Some made obscene comments about their note.

Kameron began to think his idea was not so great and wished he had never done it.

Get in a group or with a partner and unpack this case study.

Discuss what Kameron could have done differently to make a more significant impact. What are alternative ways students could have reacted?

_____
_____
_____
_____
_____
_____
_____
_____
_____
_____

Be a Bucket Filler

ACTIVITY ✎

Create a one minute and thirty-second commercial that discusses the importance of Being a Bucket Filler. Your commercial should include terms such as inclusive, mindful, self-reflection, responsible decision- making, differing cultures, healthy relationships (these are just a few examples). Be creative and thoughtful of others.

_____

_____

_____

_____

_____

_____

_____

Personal Accountability

Having Personal Accountability is such a great practice to live by. When you tell someone they have an attitude, keep in mind that an attitude results from an individual's thoughts and feelings. Personal Accountability challenges your outlook or thoughts on a comment, an action, an event, and so forth. However, choosing your attitude holds you accountable for your' and only your actions and thoughts in reaction to something.

Choosing your attitude gives you the power.

When you choose to take accountability of your choices, you take responsibility for how you respond to what life throws at you. Your choices affect others. Ask yourself: "Is my attitude helping myself, my peers, or this situation? Is it helping me to be the person I want to be?"

Being self-aware is a great skill to continue developing and supporting yourself when you choose your attitude. Being self-aware helps you to understand your strengths and things that are a little more challenging for you. If you know your triggers, you can choose to remove yourself from certain situations (if possible). Having the power of self-awareness may also aid in identifying your emotions and being aware of the emotions of others around you.

At the intersection of accountability and self-awareness, you must examine your prejudices and biases. Biases may derive from your upbringing by way of generations that may have been biased towards certain ethnic groups for different reasons. Sometimes these beliefs have been imprinted upon your subconscious or considered a part of your deep culture. Such generational beliefs may exhibit stereotypical thinking or ideas that may cause you to uphold unfair thought processes subconsciously. We must remember biases are typical, and we all have them. However, we must acknowledge our biases and be open to alternate narratives as individuals. Oftentimes our prejudice toward a situation, a group, a culture, political views, religious beliefs, and so much more, can cloud our thoughts and emotions and result in not choosing a better attitude for ourselves. This is when some self-reflection time is needed. Check yourself!

Everyone has their own unique qualities including you. Just because you do not agree with something or someone does not mean you have to have a negative attitude towards that person or group. This is a great time to be accountable, and choose a better attitude.

Personal Accountability

Dictionary.com defines **attitude** as a settled way of thinking or feeling about someone or something, typically one that is reflected in a person's behavior.

Psychology Today defines **bias** as a tendency, inclination, or prejudice toward or against something or someone.

The University of California, San Francisco Office of Diversity and Outreach defines **bias** as a prejudice in favor of or against one thing, person, or group compared with another, usually in a way that's considered unfair. Biases may be held by an individual, group, or institution and can be negative or positive.

Unconscious Bias (Implicit Bias)

According to **OSU Kirwan Institute for the Study of Race and Ethnicity**, **implicit bias** refers to the attitudes or stereotypes that affect our understanding, actions, and decisions in an unconscious manner.

Stanford Encyclopedia of Philosophy Research on **"implicit bias"** suggests that people can act based on prejudice and stereotypes without intending to do so.

> ### TIME TO DREAM
> - What are some of your triggers?
> - Discuss a time when your biases stopped you from choosing a better attitude.
> - Discuss how your attitude affects others.

Having **Personal Accountability**. It starts with intentions and awareness. You choose your attitude the moment you wake up. Is it a conscious choice or are you on autopilot? Ask yourself, "Who do I want to be today? What impact do I want to have?"

When you are aware of your choice, you control your attitude—it doesn't control you.

Name three benefits of personal accountability.

1. _____
2. _____
3. _____

Why is it important to check your biases as it relates to personal accountability?

_____
_____
_____
_____

Describe a time when you have been impacted negatively by someone else's attitude:

_____
_____
_____
_____

When people's beliefs or actions do not match yours, do you respect their differences? Does this trigger your attitude to be negative? Give an example.

_____
_____
_____
_____

How do stereotypes impact you as an individual, and how do you perceive others that are unlike you? How can this affect your attitude?

_____
_____
_____
_____

Personal Accountability

VOCABULARY

Review the vocabulary and definitions and create your own sentence to help you better understand the terms.

word	sentence

The Four Foundational Habits of a Dream Builder

CASE STUDY

Belinda was having a discussion with some classmates during study hall about their fifth bell Social Studies teacher Mr. Watkins. They were discussing whether or not his comments were appropriate or they were just biased. Belinda is a twelfth-grade student, but her study hall consists of students in grades tenth through twelfth grade. So there were other students who entered the discussion aside from her classmates. Her Social studies class was discussing the different ways immigrants are treated upon entrance into the United States. Mr. Watkins, a former immigrant, insisted that the process was easy for most immigrants based on his experience. A student named Daven in Belinda's class disagreed with Mr. Watkins because he said there were many immigrants in his family who still have not been able to get into the country and were treated poorly. This caused a huge debate which poured over into study hall and started another debate. The next day Belinda walked into class extremely upset with the way the discussion was going. During the continued discussion, Belinda shouted at Mr. Watkins and said his opinions were grossly unfair and stormed out of the classroom.

Get in a group or with a partner and unpack this case study.

What are some things you notice and wonder about this case study? What are some of the biases being presented in this scenario? In what ways could Mr. Watkins discuss his lived experiences with the class and remain open-minded? How could Belinda have expressed herself differently?

_____
_____
_____
_____
_____
_____
_____
_____
_____
_____
_____
_____

Personal Accountability

ACTIVITY ✎

(a) Choose an issue that is going on in your school or community that has caused a lot of people to feel negative about. Create a resolution to the issue(s) and present it to your class or school leaders. Be creative on how you present your information. You can create a slideshow or use a movie maker and create a commercial (these are just a couple of ideas). Be sure to get a balanced perspective on the issue. You may interview different people to get a leveled view.

(b) Create posters to display around your school and community that promotes Choosing a Positive Attitude. Be sure to include some of the vocabulary discussed in this chapter (Personal Accountability).

GLOSSARY

Be Present - To be emotionally present for people. A powerful message of respect that improves communication and strengthens relationships.

Be Present - To provide or be available to provide support to one.

Bias - Psychology Today defines bias as a tendency, inclination, or prejudice toward or against something or someone.

Case Study - An intensive study about a person, a group of people or a unit aimed to generalize and discuss findings.

Implicit Bias - According to OSU Kirwan Institute for the Study of Race and Ethnicity implicit bias refers to the attitudes or stereotypes that affect our understanding, actions, and decisions in an unconscious manner.

Implicit Bias - Stanford Encyclopedia of Philosophy Research on "implicit bias" suggests that people can act on the basis of prejudice and stereotypes without intending

Be a Bucket Filler - Finding simple ways to serve or delight people in a meaningful, memorable way.

Be Engaged & Have Fun - Engaging in activities for enjoyment and recreation rather than a serious or practical purpose.

Relationship Skills - The abilities to establish and maintain healthy relationships and to effectively navigate settings with diverse individuals and groups.

Personal Accountability - The abilities to make caring and constructive choices about personal behavior and social interaction across diverse situations.

Self-Awareness - The ability to see yourself clearly and objectively through reflection and introspection.

Self-Awareness - The abilities to understand one's own emotions, thoughts, and values and how they influence behaviors across contexts.

Self-Discipline - The ability to control one's feelings and overcome one's weaknesses; the ability to pursue what one thinks is right despite temptations to abandon it.

Self-Management - The abilities to manage one's emotions, thoughts, and behaviors effectively and to achieve goals and aspirations.

Social and Emotional Learning (SEL) - Social and Emotional Learning as the process through which children and adults acquire and effectively apply the knowledge, attitudes, and skills necessary to understand and manage emotions, set and achieve positive goals, feel and show empathy for others, establish and maintain positive relationships, and make responsible decisions.

Social Awareness - The abilities to understand the perspective and socialize with others, including those from diverse backgrounds, cultures, and contexts.

REFERENCES

CASEL (2022). Social-Emotional Learning. Retrieved from: https://casel.org/what-is-sel/

Love, L. B. (2019). We want to do more than survive: abolitionist teaching and the pursuit of educational freedom. Boston/ USA: Beacon Press.

Positive Psychology. (2022). Self-Awareness. Retrieved from: https://positivepsychology.com/self-awareness-matters-how-you-can-be-more-self-aware/

Relationship Skills. Retrieved from: https://www.definitions.net/definition/relationship+skills#:~:text=Editors%20Contribution-,relationship%20skills,and%20evolve%20with%20each%20other.

Kirwan Institute for the Study of Race and Ethnicity (2020). OSU. Retrieved from: https://kirwaninstitute.osu.edu/

Psychology Today. (2022). Bias. Retrieved from: https://www.psychologytoday.com/us/basics/bias

San Francisco Office of Diversity and Outreach. (2020) bias. Retrieved from: https://diversity.ucsf.edu/resources/unconscious-bias

Self-Awareness, Retrieved from: https://www.merriam-webster.com/dictionary/self-awareness

Made in the USA
Columbia, SC
15 June 2024